Honku

Aaron Naparstek

Honku

The Zen Antidote to Road Rage

Villard Ⓥ *New York*

A haiku from our lawyers:

This book is neither
endorsed, sponsored, nor condemned
by a carmaker

Library of Congress Cataloging-in-Publication Data
Naparstek, Aaron.
Honku: the Zen antidote to road rage / Aaron Naparstek.
p. cm.
ISBN 1-4000-6026-5
1. Automobile driving—Poetry.   2. Road rage—Prevention—Poetry.
3. Haiku, American.   I. Title.
PS3601.A63H66 2003
811'.6—dc21   2003041078

Villard Books website address: www.villard.com

Printed in the United States of America on acid-free paper

9 8 7 6 5 4 3 2

First Edition

Book design by Judith Stagnito Abbate / ABBATE DESIGN

For Joanne

This road—

no one goes down it,

autumn evening

[*Basho*]

I started writing Honku after a near-death egg-throwing experience around Christmas 2001. At the time, I lived in a one-bedroom apartment on a quintessential, historic Brooklyn street lined by trees and brownstones with big front stoops. Thanks to defects in traffic-signal timing and the brains of New York City motorists, there had always been a lot of horn honking in front of my building. But this one day it got to be too much.

Some jerk in a crappy blue sedan had decided to let loose with a continuous, nonstop blast directly beneath my window. I'd never heard anything quite like it. As the honk persisted, I felt my chest tighten and my reptilian fight-or-flight response kick in. I looked outside to see what the problem was. Not only was there no emergency, the traffic light in front of him was red!

I'd had enough. I thought to myself, if this guy is still on the horn in the amount of time it takes me to go to the fridge, get a carton of eggs, and open my window, he's getting it on the windshield. And I want him to know it was me.

My first egg hit his trunk and the second hit the top of his car with a satisfying thud that managed to break the sustained honk. But I had determined that egg-on-windshield was the just punishment for his crime. By the time the third yolk met glass, he was out of his car and he was going ballistic.

A Brooklynite of indeterminate ethnicity—stocky, balding, fortyish—he gestured toward my third-floor window, shouting, "I'm coming back tonight, *@#$&! I'm gonna kill you! I know where you live!" His sincerity was terrifying. The traffic in front of him finally began to move, but he didn't care. He just stood there screaming while the cars behind him went berserk and started blasting their horns at him.

The honker drove off and, thankfully, I never heard from him again. But the incident left me shaken. For the next couple of days I couldn't concentrate. I found myself milling about my apartment, taking stock of household items that would make good weapons. This ball-peen hammer? No, wait, the bread knife! I went to bed with a big steel monkey wrench next to my pillow.

I realized that I had snapped. I had crossed a line. I had soaked up so much honking and road rage that I had *become* the honking. I had become the rage. Though my righteous, egg-flinging fury felt sweet and just, my angry response served only to escalate the cycle of frustration and honk-violence. It only made things worse. But I couldn't take it anymore. I had to do something. So, a few weeks later, after pacing through another particularly rotten day of horn blasting, I sat down and came up with my first batch of honku—haiku poems about honking.

A haiku, as usually written in America, consists of three lines totaling seventeen syllables arranged in a 5-7-5 format. Traditionally, a good haiku makes a simple and direct observation of something in nature that leads to a Zen "Aha!" moment and a larger observation about the world as a whole. This is the moment my first honku captured:

You from New Jersey
honking in front of my house
in your SUV

I printed up copies and went out late one night taping them to lampposts up and down my street. Writing and posting my first honku felt great. Though I didn't think it would do much of anything to solve the problem, it gave me a strange sense of power over the honkers. Now, whenever I encountered an obnoxious driver, instead of muttering wrathfully to myself, I'd try to observe the scene dispassionately and construct a honku about it. It turned moments of annoyance into flashes of clarity, perspective, and amusement. I'd seemingly invented a new form of automotive anger management.

So, every couple of weeks I'd sneak out around midnight and honk back in my own quiet way:

Oh, forget Enron
the problem around here is
all the damn honking

Smoking cigarettes
blasting Hot97
futilely honking

Terrorism is
a Lincoln Continental
leaning on the horn

On the evening of my third lamppost publishing run, a woman walking her dog approached and asked excitedly if I was the "Bard of Clinton Street." When I told her I was, she extended her hand and said, "I love your work." As I made my way down the block I noticed that a handful of new honku had appeared on the lampposts, written by others. And they were good!

> *Oh, jeezus chrysler*
> *what's all the damned honking ford?*
> *please shut the truck up!*

> *They say vibrations*
> *effect energetic self*
> *honk therefore I am*

> *What keeps me from just*
> *pelting your honking auto*
> *with rotting garbage?*

In the next few weeks, dozens of honku spontaneously appeared around the neighborhood. I created a Honku.org website. Our local City Council member took up the issue. Even the people who hated the honku and thought all us complainers should move to Connecticut were posting their diatribes in 5-7-5. Soon, cops from the 76th Precinct were handing out "Please Stop Honking" flyers, along with $125 tickets to offenders.

Then I hit the elite liberal media trifecta. Almost simultaneously, the story of honku appeared in *The New Yorker*, *The New York Times*, and on NPR. From there it rapidly spread to newspapers in far-off lands such as Scotland, Sweden, and Minnesota. For the first time in years, six A.M. passed without my sleep being shattered by cabs honking their way into Manhattan. Honku was a movement! Not only did it soothe my own unique form of Brooklyn road rage, it seemed to be encouraging change as well.

Lord knows, I'm not the only one who could use some soothing change. America is going bonkers in the driver's seat. Collectively, we'll spend 3.9 billion hours stalled in traffic next year. Rush "hour" is now an all-day affair. Our vehicles are getting bigger and our parking spots fewer. Fuel prices are at historic highs, while in the most congested cities—Los Angeles, Seattle, Washington, D.C.—gridlocked drivers idle away as much as a hundred gallons a year each. The costs of maintaining our autocentric American lifestyle are becoming unbearable in all sorts of ways. One of those costs is road rage. It's endemic. Have you heard the one about the retired bookkeeper who shot and killed a guy on a Massachusetts interstate with a razor-tipped hunting arrow fired from a crossbow? It's getting medieval out there.

Meanwhile, the automotive dreamscape we see on TV grows ever further from the day-to-day reality of schlepping the kids to soccer practice. No wonder we're all so pissed off. The ads promise the freedom of a rugged SUV romping atop pristine mountains. You shelled out $45,000 for a piece of *that*, not to spend all day limping through traffic to get to the lousy job you need to pay off your expensive vehicle. The only thing standing between you and the promise of unlimited power, freedom, and mobility is that moron blocking the intersection. So, what do you do? You do the same thing the guy behind you is doing: you blast your horn. In your car, the honker is your only voice, the only form of self-expression you've got.

That is, until now! Not only does this book give you something to read during the thirty to sixty hours it's estimated you'll be stuck in traffic next year, it provides you with a fantastic new creative outlet. The next time someone steals your parking spot, cuts you off on the freeway, or flips you the bird for no good reason, don't just sit and stew (though that's better than pulling out your crossbow). Write a honku. Separate yourself from the moment of rage, observe the thing that's making your blood boil, and crystallize the experience into a pithy little 5-7-5 gem. It sounds crazy. But it worked for me.

[Acknowledgments]

Thanks first to Annie-B, Paul and Jack, the Tomlinsons, Pat Howell and son, Kate and Becca, and all of the other neighborhood people who wrote and posted their own honku. Thanks also to Craig Hammerman of Community Board 6, Captain Thomas Harris and the officers of the 76th Precinct, Councilman Bill DeBlasio, Rachel Amar and the 39th District staff, Tara George, Nick Paumgarten, Maggie Farley, Josh Deth, Clarence Eckerson, Vivian Siu, Elizabeth Puccini and Loren Runnels, Curtis Fox, Erik Schurink, Rita and Emma, One Ring Zero, Deborah Locke, Mary Lou Finlay and Barbara Budd, Lenore Skenazy, Oliver Burkeman, Doug Rushkoff, Lorretta Barrett, Susan Hobson, Jim Kunstler, Tom Gilroy, Marc Scholes, Andy Goldman, Charlie Gross, Ben Cooley, Jono Glick, Mark Landsman, Seth Safier, Niraj Sehgal, John Kaehny and every-

[Acknowledgments]

one at Transportation Alternatives (especially the Brooklyn Committee), the monks of Dai Bosatsu Zendo, Charlie Komanoff, Doug Mayer and the folks at the NPR *Car Talk* section of Cars.com, Iliya Fridman, Donna Bagdasarian, and Tim Farrell, Brian McLendon, and everyone at Villard. Thanks to all who wrote and posted their honku on the virtual Lamppost at www.honku.org. Much love to Mom, Dad, Abe, Keila, and Tom. Special thanks to Jean and Jordan, for helping us escape Clinton Street.

Honku

There are only three

types of drivers—the morons,

the insane, and me

My Ford Explorer

on a never-ending quest

for a parking spot

Gruesome hit-and-run

fatalities up ahead

how awful—I'm late

Our new minivan

so many cup holders it

needs a dishwasher

Lawyer on cell phone—

tries corporate and freeway

mergers at same time

High-beam torturer

back there in the Grand Marquis

is your name de Sade?

Drove six hours to

the Mall of America

got some McNuggets

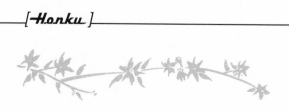

Went for oil change

got transmission, clutch, muffler—

bye-bye, Oahu

When the light turns green

like a leaf on a spring wind

the horn blows quickly

Senior citizen

45 in the left lane

needs a Viagra

The deer leaps, eyes wide

freezes in headlights—too late—

venison tonight

Sharp turn to the right—

sixty-ounce Super Big Gulp

winds up in my shoe

Silicon Valley

ten percent unemployment

traffic's much better

Morning forecast says:

It's another "bad air day"—

so try not to breathe

LAX pickup

Dante never mentioned this

tenth circle of hell

You know traffic's bad

when you envy the *hombre*

selling oranges

Do you drive it or

use it for prostate exams—

what is a Ford Probe?

Natural rhythms

moons and tides supplanted by

yellow, red, and green

Alaska's melting—

hope your Yukon Denali

doubles as a boat

If you really love

America, hang that flag

on a bicycle

Five hundred dollars

for a lousy muffler job—

I smell boat payment

Stall, rust, ping, sputter

sleazy rat-faced dealer says,

"Yeah, they all do that."

April signs of spring—

nesting doves, blossoming trees,

blood-spattered roadkill

Four-wheel-drive pickup

I remember his last words—

"Hold my beer, watch this . . ."

That's right, nosepicker

the way you are in your car

is the way you are

Guy in SUV

throws gum wrapper out window—

I throw it back in

Ford, GM, Chrysler

zero-percent financing—

great deal: more traffic

Dad, are we there yet?

About five minutes later . . .

Dad, are we there yet?

Labor Day traffic

it's flowing—we're not stopping

pee in the bottle

Just one more exit

gas prices will be lower—

cheapskate starts walking

Highway signs tell of

food, gas, lodging, and pervert—

an Amber Alert!

Need a few days off

after Sunday-night drive from

the vacation house

Gas brake gas brake gas

will you please make up your mind?

damn student driver

Aggro tailgate man

next time make it a *grande*

Prozacaccino

"Certified Pre-owned"

a fancy way of saying

it's just a used car

Thank you for sharing

your enthusiasm for

the new Eminem

Just got my license

adulthood, power, freedom

let's go to the mall

Minivan jungle—

an aggressive soccer mom

steals my parking spot

Washington, D.C.

capital of the free world

and of potholes too

Was my car stolen

or did it get towed—dammit

what's the difference?

Seething in gridlock

bike-borne I pass you, each block

we do the same dance

Other driver swerves

I give him the finger and

he shows me his gun

Defrost or a/c?

difficult to decipher

dashboard hieroglyphs

Scalding pleather seat—

no problem, I'll drive myself

to the burn unit

Morning commuters

follow measured lines, honking—

how like geese we are

Seattle traffic—

the one thing capable of

stopping Microsoft

If, in fact, TOMRULZ

would he need to announce it

on vanity plates?

Sign says 65

speedometer 130

God bless USA

Atlanta traffic

easy to see why Sherman

burned this city down

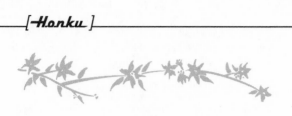

Soaring gas prices

OPEC, can you hear my cries?

praying for price wars

Is it you or me

victim of insanity

honker or honkee?

Screaming sirens pass

crap—now my ears are bleeding

call an ambulance

Psycho behind me

what do you want me to do—

hit the crossing child?

Check engine light on

unscrew dash and stab with pen—

check engine light off

That custom paint job

must have been real expensive—

bird droppings were free

Traffic camera casts

your unlucky ass in the

Ran-a-Red-Light Show

All claim innocence

in line at the impound lot

above, wing'd pigs soar

After four-hour wait

she says, "Smile!" for my photo—

fucking DMV

Gas-guzzler flying

little American flags—

the Saudis thank you

Together again

at the stoplight—was it worth

all of the speeding?

I let you over

now where is my thank-you wave?

Honda Uncivic

The morning commute

a funeral procession

each drives his own hearse

All day in the van—

pick up the kids, bring them back,

stay-at-home mom? Nope

Is it profiling

to say, "Dude in the Hummer

is an idiot"?

Our urban fabric—

the cheap upholstery of

traffic engineers

Built an interstate

through the middle of downtown—

slums sprung like mushrooms

A sign up ahead—

NOW ENTERING DELAWARE

Ha! And now? Leaving

The tow truck arrives

"That will be eighty bucks please"—

E is for empty

Conquering mountains

in TV ads this tough truck

in real life—traffic

Electric windows

were sweet, but now we desire

heated leather seats

Blaring all night long

damn car alarm—might as well

steal his radio

Ignorant boyfriend—

honking in the driveway does

not impress my dad

Nearly ran me down

then flipped me the bird as well—

welcome to Boston

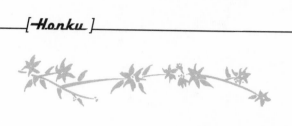

The "Big Dig" nightmare

roads open, then closed? figures—

they drink on the job

McDonald's drive-thru

a coffin with your fries, sir?

yeah, super-size it

On the bus homeward

cars with single occupants

delay my dinner

The evening sun sets

white moon journeys up the sky

I'm still in traffic

Turbulent flight home—

way less terrifying than

cab to JFK

I hear in New York

shortest distance in time is

from green light to honk

That NO PARKING sign

wasn't there when I pulled in—

now a ticket is

Though it's impressive

your vehicle's sound system

triggered my migraine

Bells and whistles ring

breaking the still night silence

who's alarmed? sleepers

Roadside pheasant waits

for my car to round the bend

for his final run

Toyota Prius

great mileage but squashed by a

Chevy Suburban

The evolution

of cars is stuck in reverse—

dinosaurs now rule

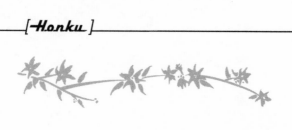

An SUV ad

featuring an F-16—

it's carmageddon

Let's see Dale Earnhardt

apply lipstick at this speed—

NASCAR mommy-style

Call search and rescue

my daughter's lost inside our

Ford Expedition

I saw that finger!

yes, you in the Intrepid—

we shall meet again

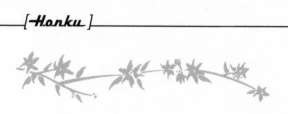

Horse trailer ahead

penalty for tailgating—

horse pies on my hood

Midlife-crisis man

trade in that sports car for some

psychotherapy

A scolded driver

apologizes to us—

only in Berkeley

Hot 'n' heavy in

the backseat of Dad's sedan

college dreams . . . buh-bye

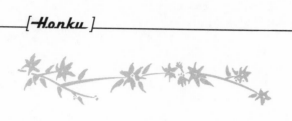

Men: would rather pay

thousands for GPS than

ask for directions

Oh, Mister Softee

your jingling so relentless

pop goes my weasel

The air in Houston—

too darn thick to breathe but our

sunsets look pretty

Cabbie's sharp swift stench

fells a tiny forest of

pine-tree fresheners

Ah, New York, New York,

those horns are stressing me out—

stop spreadin' the news

New alternator—

in 70,000 miles

this one will die too

Aerodynamics—

seriously compromised

by splattering bugs

Let the forest burn

the Toyota Sequoia

continues to grow

Hollywood and Vine

friggin' jerk just cut me off—

    cool, it's Martin Sheen!

Driver's license fee—

deal! save eight dollars if you

donate an organ

Damn rubberneckers!

an hour in traffic till I

got my turn to look

Stop signs all four ways

since everyone is stopping

guess I don't have to

I'm writing haiku

going eighty miles per hour—

is that safe to do?

[Contributors]

Thanks to the following people for contributing lines, phrases, and complete honku to this book: Eric Anderson, Jane Auerbach, Candice Belanoff, Aline Bernstein, Bob Bowen, James Cardillo, Val Carpenter, David Gerry Craig, Clarence Eckerson, Amy Forstadt, Michael Hearst, Ivan Held, Justine Henderson, Dick and Lisa Hurban, T. J. Jones, Amy Kunce, Mark Landsman, Bill Littlefield, Leigh McDevitt, Brian McLendon, Howard Miller, Shelly Moses, Boniface Muggli, Jean Nerenberg, Joanne Nerenberg, Jim Phripjah, Ali Rushfield, Terry Ryan, Michael J. Smith, Mike and Vicki Stroeher, Liz Tinney, David Tussey, Linda Wallace, Tim Ward, Jason Wentworth, and the staff of *Car Talk* on NPR.

Thanks to all of the great honkuists who contributed poems, discussion and ideas to my website, **www.honku.org**.

───────────{ *About the Author* }───

AARON NAPARSTEK is a writer and interactive media producer in Brooklyn, New York. He and his fiancée, Joanne, recently moved from their honk-ridden apartment to a nice old town house with a big oak tree in the backyard, where, instead of waking to car horns, they arise each morning to the sound of chirping birds. Now, about those damn birds . . .